GET A JOB

AT THE

GROCERY STORE

DIANE LINDSEY REEVES

Created and produced by
Bright Futures Press, Cary, North Carolina
www.brightfuturespress.com

Published by
Cherry Lake Publishing, Ann Arbor, Michigan
www.cherrylakepublishing.com

Photo Credits: cover, Shutterstock/mmkarabella; page 4, Shutterstock/Pierre Desrosiers; page 5, Shutterstock/
bikeriderlondon; page 7, Shutterstock/Pointimages; page 7, Shutterstock/Alison Hancock; page 9, Shutterstock/Tyler
Olson; page 11, Shutterstock/goodluz; page 11, Shutterstock/hodff; page 13, Shutterstock/XiXinXing; page 15, Shutterstock/
science photo; page 15, Shutterstock/MOLPIX; page 17, Shutterstock/Menno Schaefer; page 19, Shutterstock/Ratthaphong
Ekariyasap; page 19, Shutterstock/Free Prod33; page 21, Shutterstock/Kzenon; page 23, Shutterstock/Elnur; page 23,
Shutterstock/Smart art; page 25, Shutterstock/Kzenon; page 27, Shutterstock/Studio Smile; page 27, Shutterstock/Aleph
Studio; page 28, Shutterstock/Pressmaster.

Illustrated by Chris Griffin

Library of Congress Cataloging-in-Publication Date

CIP data has been filed and is available at catalog.loc.gov.

Printed in the United States of America

TABLE OF CONTENTS

If there is one thing Job likes, it is food!

Like most people, he eats morning, noon, and night. Pizza, of course, is one of his favorite foods. Of the approximately 3 billion pizzas sold in the United States each year, Job estimates that he eats about half of them!

Okay, that might be a slight exaggeration. But still...

Job is a fictional kid named **J**eremiah **O**liver **B**aumgartner. His initials are J.O.B., so his friends call him Job for short. His parents think it's the perfect nickname, because it's hard work having a kid like Job. It's not that Job is a troublemaker. He's a great kid. But trouble seems to go out of its way to find him. And when Job gets hungry, trouble turns into double trouble.

When he and his dad go to the supermarket to restock his family's kitchen shelves, Job makes new discoveries about how food gets there. Come along with Job as he works up an appetite at the local grocery store. While he explores the aisles, you can explore the different jobs people do to fill grocery store shelves with the delicious foods we all love to eat.

FOOD BITE
An estimated 3.4 million employees work in U.S. supermarkets.

What did the lettuce say
to the celery?
Are you stalking me?

Produce managers run the produce departments at local supermarkets. It's their job to keep this section well-stocked with fresh fruits and veggies. They manage the department's inventory, staff, pricing, and promotions. Produce managers are also responsible for creating and maintaining produce displays. They pay special attention to which foods can be displayed at room temperature and which foods must be refrigerated. Since the produce department is where many shoppers begin their grocery shopping, produce managers want to make a good first impression.

THE RESULTS

Job was hungry and grumpy when he and his dad arrived at the supermarket. So Job's dad decided to make a game out of the shopping trip.

"Let's start in the produce section and get the fruits and veggies," Job's dad suggested. "This stuff comes from all over the world. I'll get the apples and oranges. You find something that came from a place you would like to visit someday."

At first, Job didn't get it. Then he started noticing the signs next to each item. Bananas from Mexico. Potatoes from Idaho. And pineapple—Job's favorite fruit—from Hawaii.

"Aloha!" Job said, as he dropped a pineapple into the shopping cart.

CHAPTER 2
JOB MEETS MEAT

9

"So, we 'meat' again," Job grinned, as they rounded the corner into the meat department.

Job's dad answered with another pun. "It is nice to 'meat' you."

"Yeah," Job said. "Hope to see you again soon so we can 'ketchup.'"

Job and his dad were laughing so hard at their own jokes, they almost forgot to get the pork chops.

A **rancher** owns or manages a ranch where livestock is raised. Cows are raised and sold as meat. Sheep are raised for their wool. Ranchers spend most of their workday outdoors. They herd animals from pasture to pasture and take care of the fences and grounds. Ranchers work closely with veterinarians to keep their herds healthy and often assist in the birth of animals, as well as the **branding** and **tagging**. Ranchers may grow hay, corn, alfalfa, and other pasture plants to supplement the grass that herds graze on. Ranchers also handle the business aspects of their ranches.

Butchers use sharp tools such as knives, grinders, and meat saws to prepare the different cuts of meat sold in a grocery store. This includes steaks, roasts, and a variety of ground meats. Keeping their work area safe and super clean is a top priority for butchers. They weigh, package, and label meat products for sale to consumers. Butchers sometimes provide cooking instructions and other useful tips to store customers.

Ranchers keep their cattle well-fed.

USDA food inspectors work for the United States Department of Agriculture (USDA) and inspect the foods that American consumers eat. They are knowledgeable about federal laws and regulations that govern food products. They inspect food manufacturers, distributors, and processors to make sure that work environments are clean and food products are safe to eat. President Abraham Lincoln established the USDA in 1862 to protect American citizens from the dangers of eating rotten or diseased foods.

Meat clerks work in the meat departments of grocery stores. They are responsible for weighing, wrapping, and pricing meat products for customers. Some meat clerks may be responsible for slicing meats sold in the deli department and often work directly with customers to

Butchers prepare many cuts of meat.

Food Bite

It is estimated that the average American meal travels 1,500 miles (2,414 kilometers) to get from farm to plate.

fulfill their orders. It is their job to keep the work area and the display counters clean. They also check to see that the meats on display are fresh and discard products that are past their sell-by dates.

The Results

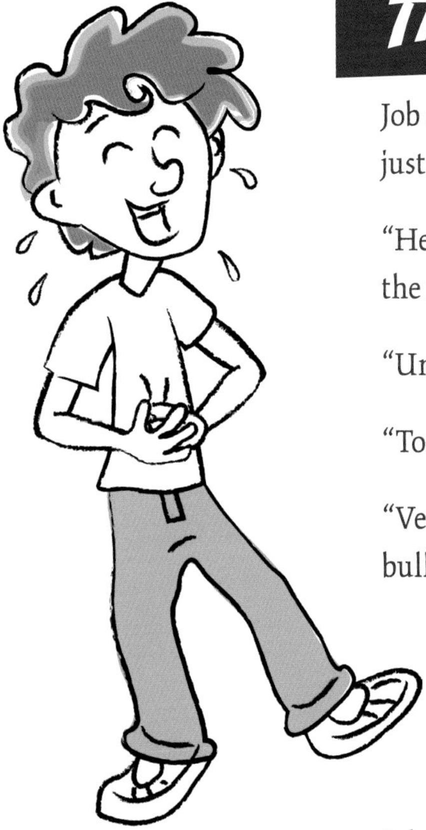

Job and his dad were on a roll with the corny jokes. They just couldn't stop themselves.

"Hey, Dad," Job asked with a grin. "Why did the cow cross the road?"

"Um, beats me," his dad answered.

"To get to the udder side!" Job laughed. "Get it? Udder side?"

"Very funny," his dad said. "What do you call a sleeping bull?"

"That's easy," Job said. "A bull-dozer!"

"Okay, try this one," Job's dad said, determined to stump him. "Where do cows go for entertainment?"

Job was puzzled. "Where?"

"To the moo-vies!"

CHAPTER 3
JOB PICKS UP SOME PACKAGED FOOD

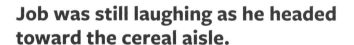

Job was still laughing as he headed toward the cereal aisle.

He was laughing so hard that he didn't notice the big display of Funky Fruit Flakes around the corner.

Kaboom!

His shopping cart went one way. Job went the other way. And the cereal boxes went every which way.

"Oops!" Job said. How embarrassing!

Job handed a box of his favorite cereal to his dad. "I guess we can mark breakfast cereal off the shopping list now."

Food scientists use chemistry, biology, and other sciences to study the basic elements of food. They determine its nutritional content, create new products, and research ways to make processed foods safe and healthy. Many food scientists work for companies that manufacture packaged foods like cereals, granola bars, potato chips, and other snack foods. Others help manufacturing companies figure out the best ways to process and package foods.

Packaging engineers design and construct the boxes, cartons, bottles, and other containers holding the foods that are for sale. Packaging engineers must design solutions that keep foods fresh and protected. They must also consider how food will be displayed in stores. There are lots of products to look at when grocery shopping. Packaging engineers want to make sure their packaging gets customers' attention.

There are many different ways that **nutritionists** work in the food and beverage industry. Some develop new products and recipes in test kitchens. Others analyze and create the nutrition information included on food labels. Nutritionists might also inspect products as they are manufactured to make sure that government standards are followed. All nutritionists work to make food choices safer and healthier for consumers.

Nutritionists analyze the nutritional value of foods.

Food manufacturers use **automation** to process foods. Automation is the use of machines to make products. Sometimes robots are involved in the manufacturing process! Processing makes food more convenient to prepare and preserves food longer. Food manufacturers determine the most effective ways to freeze, can, refrigerate, or dehydrate fresh foods. Many of the packaged foods found on grocery store shelves and in the freezer section have been processed in one way or another.

Getting the food from farms, through the processing plants, and out to grocery stores involves many different

Automation makes the food production process quicker and more efficient.

jobs. The **supply chain** process includes people who work in factories and warehouses, in **logistics**, and in transportation. Food is moved by ships, trucks, and railroads. If you could follow a box of cereal from the fields where the grains are grown to your local grocery store, you would have quite an adventure!

Wow! Is this cereal or a chemistry set?

THE RESULTS

"What is cereal made of, anyway?" Job wondered.

He picked up a box and looked at the list of ingredients. Among other things, the label listed maltose, tripotassium phosphate, tocopherol, and folic acid.

"Ick! I think I just lost my appetite," Job mumbled.

Job's dad looked at the label.

"Those are the additives that keep cereal fresh and give it more flavor," his dad said.

"Let's look for a cereal that has more ingredients I recognize," Job suggested.

CHAPTER 4

JOB DARES TO CHOOSE DAIRY

Next on the shopping list was milk.

In the big refrigerators in the dairy section, Job found milk from cows, goats, coconuts, almonds, soy, and rice. There was whole milk, skim milk, low-fat milk, buttermilk, and chocolate milk. Some of the labels said "organic." Others said "hormone-free."

So many choices! How was Job supposed to know which kind to get?

He stared at the choices for a while. Then he did what any kid in his shoes would do.

"Eeny, meeny, miney, mo …"

A **dairy farmer** owns or manages a farm where animals are raised to produce milk. The average herd size on a dairy farm is 187 cows. Every morning and every evening, those cows have to be milked. One cow produces 6 to 8 gallons (23 to 30 liters) of milk each day. That's a lot of milk in one day from one farm! Milking is a time-intensive process, but farmers don't have to milk cows by hand anymore. Up to 100 cows can be milked at once using milking machines.

Milk tanker drivers transport milk from the dairy farms to the factories where it is **pasteurized** and made ready for sale to stores. Milk tankers are made of stainless steel and keep milk cold while it is being transported to the factory. The drivers are trained to check the quality of the milk they collect. They do not take milk that doesn't look or smell right.

Large animal veterinarians travel from farm to farm taking care of cows, horses, sheep, and other livestock. A big part of their job is keeping animals in the food chain healthy. They do this by giving vaccinations, providing health exams, and treating illnesses. They draw blood, clean and close up wounds, and prescribe medicines. They also assist in birthing animals. These vets often drive specially outfitted trucks that let them bring medical care to farms were animal care is needed.

Milking machines allow farmers to milk many cows at once.

Cheese is made from milk and comes in a wide variety of flavors, textures, and forms. Some **cheese makers** work for large companies that make the processed cheeses you find in a grocery store's dairy department. They use computers and machines to make enormous amounts of cheese. Their focus is on quality control, developing new products,

Cheese is made from the milk of cows, goats, and sheep.

FOOD BITE

The average American consumes about 630 pounds (286 kilograms) of milk, yogurt, cheese, and ice cream a year.

and improving the cheese-making process. Other cheese makers specialize in creating smaller batches of handmade **artisan** cheese. These cheeses tend to be more expensive and of a higher quality. Many stores offer separate areas to display these fancier cheeses.

A **dairy clerk** is in charge of pricing, stocking, and rotating a grocery store's dairy products. Milks, cheeses, and ice creams have a shorter shelf life than other foods, so an important part of the job is making sure the products on display are fresh. Products past their "sell-by" dates must be removed. This job involves heavy lifting and working in refrigerated areas of the store.

THE RESULTS

Finally, Job reached his favorite part of the store—the ice cream aisle! There were so many yummy flavors that Job knew it would take time to make his choices.

They didn't call this the "frozen foods aisle" for nothing. Brrr!

Fortunately, Job came prepared …

I give these doughnuts two thumbs way up!

Job followed his nose all the way to the bakery.

That's where he discovered the baker taking doughnuts out of the big oven. Fresh baked doughnuts!

"I hope those taste as good as they smell," Job said.

He still hadn't eaten breakfast. But that situation was about to change.

"I'll take one of each," Job told the clerk.

Bakers start work very early in the morning. They have to fill bakery shelves with goodies such as cookies, cakes, and pastries in time for the morning rush of shoppers. Bakers use kitchens that are different than the ones in typical houses. These "commercial" kitchens are equipped with high-volume mixers, large ovens, and other tools they need to make big batches of lots of recipes.

Special occasions call for special cakes. **Cake decorators** decorate cakes for birthdays, weddings, holidays, and other celebrations. Some decorators add simple designs such as balloons, flowers, and greetings to the sheet cakes they sell. Others create elaborate cakes that are works of art—with shapes, designs, and decorations formed from marzipan, fondant, gum paste, and other edible materials. Wedding cakes can be especially spectacular, with multiple layers and amazing designs that take hours or even days to create.

Bakery associates work behind the counter in grocery store bakeries. They take care of customers, wrap and label goodies, and slice loaves of bread. Bakery associates may also help bakers by loading and unloading ovens and helping prepare baked goods.

Cupcakes are a fun bakery treat.

As you may know from reading the classic children's book *The Little Red Hen*, a lot goes into making flour. Someone has to grow the wheat, cut the wheat, and take the wheat to be ground into flour. Flour is one of the main ingredients in most baked goods. **Millers** work in flour mills to grind wheat into the soft, silky flours used to make cakes, cookies, and other sweets.

Mexicans eat tortillas, Middle Easterners eat pita, and Indians eat naan. Each country and culture has its own version, but for the past 30,000 years, humans everywhere have been eating bread. It is a staple that provides toast in the morning, sandwiches at

Millers grind wheat into flour.

lunch, and dinner rolls in the evening. **Bread makers** sometimes work in big commercial bakeries that supply grocery stores with millions of loaves of bread every year. Other bread artisans craft specialty breads by hand or in smaller batches. They sell these breads in independent bakeries and gourmet restaurants.

No more bare cupboard for us!

THE RESULTS

When Job's mom got home from the gym, she was impressed that Job and his dad had already put away all the groceries. Now Job was standing in front of the very full pantry. There was so much food that he was having trouble deciding what to make for lunch.

"Wow! It looks like you bought one of everything at the grocery store," Job's mom said.

"That's what happens when you send a hungry kid to the store," he said.

CHAPTER 6

WHO DOES WHAT AT THE GROCERY STORE?

WHO DOES WHAT?

Job met some interesting people during his trip to the grocery store. Can you match their job titles with the correct job descriptions?

Please do NOT write in this book if it is not yours. Use a separate piece of paper.

1. Makes sure that food processing plants meet all federal food regulations

2. Grinds wheat into flour

3. Designs the containers that keep food fresh

4. Transports milk from farms to factories in specially equipped tankers

5. Uses sharp tools to prepare cuts of meat sold in grocery stores

A. Packaging engineer

B. Milk tanker driver

C. Butcher

D. Miller

E. USDA food inspector

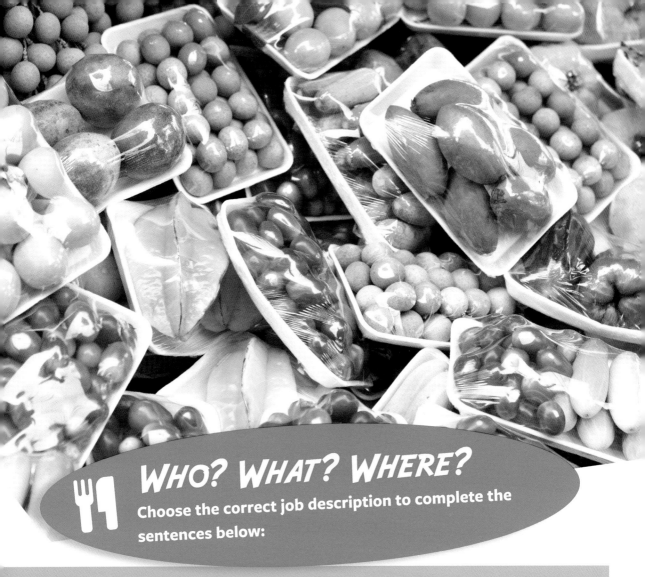

WHO? WHAT? WHERE?

Choose the correct job description to complete the sentences below:

1. _____ are sometimes referred to as "crop doctors."

2. _____ price, stock, and rotate products in the dairy section of a grocery store.

3. _____ develop new product ideas and recipes in test kitchens.

4. _____ grow crops like fruits, vegetables, and grains.

5. _____ help people celebrate special occasions with beautifully decorated cakes.

A. Nutritionists

B. Cake decorators

C. Farmers

D. Agronomists

E. Dairy clerks

Answer key: 1-D; 2-E; 3-A; 4-C; 5-B

27

CHAPTER 7
IT'S YOUR TURN

Job's visit to the grocery store turned out to be quite an adventure.

Share an experience that you or a family member had at a grocery store. Be sure to mention all the people who helped you along the way.

Pssst ... If this book doesn't belong to you, write your answers on a separate sheet of paper so you don't get in BIG trouble.

Go online to download a free activity sheet at
www.cherrylakepublishing.com/activities.

GLOSSARY

agronomist
scientist who deals with crop production and soil management

artisan
a food or drink made in a traditional or nonmechanical way using high-quality ingredients

automation
the use of machines in the manufacturing production process

baker
person who makes cakes, cookies, and other pastries

bakery associate
person who works in the bakery department of a grocery store

bread maker
person who bakes bread

butcher
person whose job is to cut up and sell meat

branding
to mark an animal with a branding iron

cake decorator
person who decorates cakes that are sold to celebrate special occasions

cheese maker
person who specializes in making cheeses

cooperative
businesses owned by all the people who work in them and who share the responsibilities and the profits

dairy clerk
person who works in the dairy department of a grocery store

dairy farmer
farmer devoted to the production of milk, butter, and cheese

distributor
a company that buys products from one company and arranges for other companies to sell them

farmer
person who owns or manages a farm

food manufacturer
person who uses automated processes to mass-produce food products

food scientist
person who studies the microbiological, physical, and chemical properties of foods

large animal veterinarian
doctor who specializes in treating farm animals

logistics
the detailed coordination of a complex operation involving many people, facilities, or supplies

meat clerk
person who works in the meat department of a grocery store

milk tanker driver
specially trained driver of the truck used to transport milk from farms to factories

miller
person who grinds wheat into flour

nutritionist
person who works to make food choices safer and healthier for consumers

packaging engineer
person who designs packaging for food and other products

pasteurized
partially sterilized to make the product safe for consumption and improve its shelf life

produce buyer
person who procures and purchases produce used by food processors or sold in grocery stores

produce manager
person who manages the produce department at a grocery store

produce sourcer
person who secures specific types of fruits and vegetables for clients such as food distributors and grocery store chains

rancher
person who owns or manages a ranch where livestock is raised

tagging
to attach a plastic or metal object used for identification of domestic livestock and other animals

supply chain
the sequence of processes involved in the production and distribution of a commodity such as food

USDA food inspector
person who inspects places where food is raised or made for the purpose of consumer safety

INDEX

ABOUT THE AUTHOR

Diane Lindsey Reeves is the author of lots of children's books. She has written several original PEANUTS stories (published by Regnery Kids and Sourcebooks). She is especially curious about what people do and likes to write books that get kids thinking about all the cool things they can be when they grow up. She lives in Cary, North Carolina, and her favorite thing to do is play with her grandkids—Conrad, Evan, Reid, and Hollis Grace.